a delicate dance of wings

a delicate dance of wings

haibun by

Linda Jeannette Ward

botanical prints by

Pamela A. Babusci

pen & ink drawings by

J. W. Stansell

A cooperative publication of

Winfred Press
&
Clinging Vine Press

a delicate dance of wings

Copyright © 2002 - 2010 by Linda Jeannette Ward
All Rights Reserved
Second Printing

Publication of this book was made possible, in part, by a grant from the North Carolina Arts Council, a State Agency.

Acknowledgment is made to the following publications where most of these haibun first appeared, some in slightly different form:

American Haibun and Haiga, Volumes I & II, black bough, Frogpond, Lynx and Modern Haiku

Cover art by Pamela A. Babusci, © 2002
Wings
Tempera Watercolor

Published by
Winfred Press
364 Wilson Hill Road
Colrain, MA 01340
winfred@crocker.com
http://larrykimmel.tripod.com/

Clinging Vine Press
P.O. Box 231
Coinjock, NC 27923
tankapoet@yahoo.com

ISBN: 0-9702457-4-2

For Sarah Wagoner

I long for wildness...woods where the wood thrush forever sings, where the hours are early morning ones, and there is dew on the grass, and the day is forever unproved....the birds I heard, sung as freshly as if it had been the first morning of creation, stretching through many a Carolina of the soul.

Henry David Thoreau

Contents

HOME

A Wilsonian Tale	5
A Moth for La Tour	7
The Horseshoe Drive	8
A Country Road	11
Legacy	12
Winter Sun	14
Woodcock	16
Laundry Day	18

OUTER BANKS

Island Sunrise	23
Whimbrel Cottage	24
Ebb Tide	27
Whimbrel Cottage Revisited	28
small time	30
Moon Watch	32
Spring Planting	35

AFIELD

City Park	39
Alligator River Wildlife Refuge	40
South Texas	43
Mesa Verde, Colorado	44
Pigeon Mountain	45
Merchants Millpond State Park, NC	49

Introduction

Haibun are short prose pieces, usually autobiographical in nature, mingled with one or more haiku, a short Japanese poem of seventeen sound units or less, portraying a moment keenly perceived; or a tanka, also a Japanese poem but using thirty-one sound units or less and written in a five line format. By autobiographical it is meant that the haibun is something the author has experienced or witnessed.

Haibun have grown out of a Japanese literary tradition exemplarized by the travel diaries of Basho, the 17th century father of the modern haiku. Of Basho's travel diaries, *The Narrow Road to the Deep North*, is the most famous and considered to be a classic work in Japanese literature. It has served and still does serve as a touchstone both to Japanese haibun and its more recent western-language equivalents.

The prose text of a haibun at its best is described as a poetic prose and also as a prose of "lightness", a quality also the ideal of the haiku, or *hokku*, as it was called in Basho's time. The relationship between the prose text of the haibun and the haiku, or tanka, that caps it are of prime importance to the defining of this form. The haiku should *extend* the text, for example, not repeat, or recapitulate, what has already been written, and if the poet-writer of a haibun can bring about a resonance that reverberates between the haiku and the prose text, this is considered the quintessence of the haibun form.

In the English-language haibun of today, we are seeing a great deal of experimentation with the haibun as new subject materials and new treatments of prose are explored. But the above "in-a-nutshell" definition of the haibun seems to persist as the fundamental tone in the contemporary fugue of exploration.

Linda Jeannette Ward, an acclaimed haiku and tanka poet, with her recently published tanka sequence, *a frayed red thread* and winner in the prestigious Harold G. Henderson Awards for 2001, stays close to the haibun tradition, with its emphasis on nature, both in its small and its large dramas, and their subsequent effect on human nature, though her brief diary-like narratives are very much in the American grain.

a delicate dance of wings, then, is a wonderfully conceived collection of true life mini-dramas as perceived and expressed by a practiced and sensitive poet-writer of the first order, bringing to life a variety of daily, as well as extraordinary, life events experienced in and through nature both at its most tranquil and its most ferocious moments.

Larry Kimmel
Colrain, Massachusetts
March 2002

HOME

A Wilsonian Tale

Biophilia, if it exists, and I believe it exists, is the innately emotional affiliation of human beings to other living organisms. Edward O. Wilson

My grandparents place: a refuge for a city-raised child, filled with woods, hidden ponds and creeks with a gravel road meandering through 300 acres. My days there filled with leisurely walks, Grandmother often accompanying me to point out black-dotted frog eggs in puddles or deer feeding on fallen persimmons in a hidden, neglected grove . . . but I'm often allowed to roam free, all by myself I explore, one day encountering a pair of turkey vultures who pause only to offer a passing glance at my approach . . . they seem so huge from my ten-year-old perspective: menacing black monsters with wrinkled necks and scrawny heads the color of the blood they feed on. Standing frozen with fright, then with fascination, I watch . . .

>road kill ~
>a delicate dance of wings
>over ripped flesh

Reminiscing now, I wonder if this chance meeting sealed my bond with the avian world, a bioaffiliation that I follow yet into old age . . .

>autumn twilight ~
>and still the whir
>of hummingbird wings

A Moth for La Tour

On the cover of the *Smithsonian* there's a painting of a gypsy girl by Georges de La Tour, a close-up shot revealing tiny cracks in the aged canvas; yet this renaissance maid appears young and fresh: her round face framed by a kerchief folded tight to her head and tied in a simple little knot under her chin, no hint of hair exposed, no wispy stray escaping. Shades of copper and rose blend together across finely cracked cheeks, her eyes portrayed in a sideways glance, engaged in trickery, the text says.

On the table beside me this magazine has mysteriously attracted a moth whose copper and rose wings perfectly match the gypsy's cheek where it rests almost camouflaged, as if the artist, weary of painting only people, had endeavored to add a touch of nature for a more rustic look.

I don't know how this tiny moth found its way inside and what instinct urged it to a surface so foreign to its natural home, yet so like its own softly colored wings. I want to leave it there, a reminder of how magic life can be . . .

> barely visible
> on her painted cheek
> rose and copper moth

THE HORSESHOE DRIVE

After long anticipation Grandma gives in to my pleas to watch from a safe distance while Grandpap's new horse is unloaded from her trailer. I've been cautioned against getting my hopes up about riding this horse—her mission is strictly utilitarian. By twelve years of age I've been told only part of the reason behind the arrival of this plain grey mare: Uncle Fulton died at sixteen, the beloved first born. By the end of this day I was to learn how . . .

    spilled blood ~
    same color as the tractor
    that killed him

The mailman discovered his body—twisted beneath Grand-pap's new Farmall tractor. Exiting his assigned field after a morning's work, Fulton entered the horseshoe drive of an adjoining churchyard, a customary turn-around spot bordered by an old cemetery with only a few vacancies for new arrivals. He failed to see the rough stones piled off to one side—a precaution against scavengers the parish sexton would use to mound over a grave consecrated the day before . . .

    gravestones ~
    one set of wheels
    spins freely in the air

Within a week after Fulton's burial Grandpap's hair turned silver white and he became the quiet man I knew . . .

    in a deserted stall
    the shiny new tractor
    deserted

Finally, without consulting anyone, Grandma arranged for a neighbor to take the tractor away. Grandpap never asked how or where . . .

> a patch of white bobs
> between furrowed rows
> the steady tread of a horse

A Country Road

The pungency of hot asphalt mixed with the scent of approaching thunder—one of those blazing midsummer days where light glows round the edges of dark bulbous clouds that bud in the distance and blossom suddenly overhead . . . a corn-colored haze wafts around our idling car, coats our windscreen with a fine layer of agricultural dust released from an overturned grain truck whose mountainous load of husked corn has spilled in yellow streams across this back country road lined with what seem to be abandoned migrant shacks: square structures of wood weathered to silver—one window, one room, one tattered screen door that opens . . .

> market day ~
> a man and a woman
> wield dustpan and broom

Legacy

Summers at my grandparents' farm: fields of tomatoes and squash, an apple orchard and woodland paths bordered by wild blueberries that lead to a clearing where a weathered barn holds frayed woven baskets and an old apple press. Deer gather along the edge of an abandoned homestead that once stood atop a hill where on sultry days Grandfather leads me down its steep bank to drink spring water so cool beads of condensation form on the jar he lifts from an earthen shelf . . .

> deep in a gully
> where a mighty force once ran
> grandpap's secret spring
> running rivulets
> down a clear Mason jar

As I neared puberty, Grandfather was diagnosed with glaucoma—too late to respond to the primitive treatment of the times . . .

> grandfather's
> memories those last years
> after his blindness:
> the red of strawberry fields
> the blue of sky
>
> how do I know
> the color of his memories?
> with open eyes
> the visions we shared
> disappear

In midlife, I learn that I've harbored his gene, but in a more fortunate era of medical science my sight is preserved, as my memory of his final days, sitting in grass, trimming it by the touch of his hand. Aware then of his grief, only now do I know how heavy the sorrowful burden he must have carried . . .

> only a little
> part of my life
> has mattered
> now I think of it
> seeing is reason enough

WINTER SUN

In mid-January we're promised several days of spring-like weather beginning today the family we've hired to replace our roof arrives just as last night's frost begins to retreat from their work space. Highly recommended by neighbors for their expeditious work they pile out from two vehicles—a battered red pickup and a glossy white compact. The head of the clan greets us wreathed in cigarette smoke, his wife's smile reveals a golden tooth next to a missing one, his daughter-in-law looks as wiry and strong as her husband—and two young men, perhaps brothers or grandsons, begin hoisting stacks of shingles onto their backs. Soon all are busy with their assigned tasks to the sound of scraping and tearing of weathered shingles that come sailing from the roof, accompanied by rounds of rhythmic hammering . . .

> roofers at work ~
> only the deaf cat
> at ease

The matriarch of the family is the only one not to ascend a ladder. Her job is to gather old shingles, bent nails and torn paper pieces into a wheelbarrow and dump each load into the bed of the pickup. While she waits for another load to pile up, she takes a break on the garden bench, her hair tucked under a watch cap and hands in the pocket of her bulky jacket she sits in the winter sun at first watching the work crew above her, then turning her attention to the small pond beside her . . .

> weather worn Buddha
> beside the lily pond
> her eyes follow golden scales

Woodcock

An overcast day in December. Cabin fever setting in early this season, too much Christmas and artificial planning, we escape into winter wraps and cross the Chesapeake Bay to Eastern Shore, Virginia, stopping to bird the manmade islands we view sea ducks from splattered rocks, the wind whipping around us, waves whipping up too. Arriving at the wildlife refuge late afternoon we find a lone ranger there, specialist in woodcock, a host for their winter home who shows us how to walk leafy brush piles, listening for the peculiar whine of their wings before we see gold and brown glimpses of birds fluttering low, only to be lost in perfect camouflage near our feet.

> from autumn leaves
> the brief glimmer
> of woodcocks

The rest of the day spent in surprise and frustration as we flush bird after bird only to have them instantly vanish. How could so many be so hard to see? At twilight we drive along the edge of a field that shelters them by day and from where our ranger says they emerge at sunset to probe the damp roadside for worms with their long, flexible bills.

> low-beam lights—
> pencil-thin shadows
> of a dozen bills

Satisfied at last, we head for home with night lights of ships bobbing alongside the Bay-bridge crossing, our talk quiet at first, then returning to woodcocks and what the ranger taught, we realize our habitat at home should be perfect—have we missed this bird in the small refuge we've tended all these years? Energy returning we're sitting alert and ready by the time we enter the tree-lined drive to our house.

> shining liquid brown
> from the tops of their heads
> the eyes of woodcocks

LAUNDRY DAY

I never knew quilts had names until my mother mailed me pictures of the ones she had made, along with a note asking me to select my favorite as a gift. I chose one called *Picket Fence*.

I always wait for warm breezy days to launder my quilt so it will dry as fluffy as it was when I first received it. I carefully place each clothespin along its border of tiny blue flowers that frame alternating shades of blue and white zig-zagging across its whole, creating the delightful picket effect. When the quilt's dry I gather it into my arms as I remove the wooden pins and carry it to the house, holding it lightly to my chest so as not to crush the fluffiness. Once inside I head straight for the bedroom and allow it to float in gentle folds upon the bed . . .

>   laundry day ~
>   over the picket fence quilt
>   a tan and black snake

OUTER BANKS

ISLAND SUNRISE

Awakened by the staccato calls of boat-tailed grackles, I find them strutting along the rail of our cottage deck, beaks stretched skyward, wingtips pointing to earth in the spring display competing males perform to attract their mates . . . ebony feathers flash shades of purple and blue as light begins to break on the horizon . . .

> on pointed beaks
> nudged higher and higher
> the morning sun

My mind pleasantly suspended in dawn's dazzling glare, an open book lies forgotten on my lap, waiting for the restless time that is gone now . . . there's only this beach, this cloudless sky and a scattering of gulls when I return my gaze to the words before me . . .

> how delicately
> she brushes
> ancient calligraphy
> . . . yellow damselfly
> upon the *Tao Te Ching*

WHIMBREL COTTAGE

For three days we're held captive in our cottage strewn with birding guides, binoculars and books while autumn's northeast winds roar and sigh up and down the beach. . . now we hear news of Josephine rushing to join us, a tropical storm spiraling up the Atlantic coast leaving Florida devastated in her wake, she heads for the Outer Banks of North Carolina, churning our ocean with her imminent attack, lining up waves in orderly rows that rise higher and higher . . .

        each cresting wave
        a glimmer of moonlight
        crashing

Weary of storm vigilance I retreat to the bedroom, flannel sheets from home swaddling me against the storm . . . a steady sea spray patters the window above my head, the floor beneath me shudders with the wind's gathering force
. . . I close my eyes, feeling strangely calmed by nature's upheaval, listening as raindrops and ocean spray merge together as though amassing tears of rage to smear the small panes of glass that frame its fury. The bed begins to rock, dispelling fears and bringing dreams of a watchful nanny's hand swaying a cradle to her soothing lullaby. . .

        barrier island
        rocking her to sleep
        a tropical storm

Our turbulent vacation over we return to home and work, only to hear news of El Nino—nor'easters to be especially hard this coming winter we watch as each weather report announces spring-like conditions—including one storm following close on another. Televised scenes of beach cottages falling into the sea appear almost weekly on our local news . . . after one record-breaking storm we venture out to visit Whimbrel Cottage, past flooded fields, wind-downed signs and stretches of empty beach where once familiar houses stood.

      storm clearing—
      atop every other house
      roofers at work

Sand in uneven layers crisscrosses cracked pavement that leads upwards to the dune we know so well . . . just beyond its rise we hope to find our cottage still standing, hope that its record of enduring fifty years of storms has held once more through a nor'easter that blew through under a full moon, pulling tides seven feet above normal . . . we come to the crest of the hill, the roar of the ocean louder now, relief washing over us when we see roof and windows intact we don't at first notice the pile of broken boards where once an outdoor shower stall stood and wooden steps led the way to our beachside retreat . . .

      shattered steps leading nowhere
      . . . seaside cottage
      marooned on the sand

With trepidation, we walk under floors we remember swaying with the same motion as a fishing pier reaching out into the sea . . . we look up at sea-sprayed windows, at a strip of exposed wood shining bright tan against the grey of weathered boards all still in place high above us, the cottage's reinforced stilts somehow holding in wet sand, yet another nor'easter is forecast in two days . . .

      heavy rain—
      an object in the next room
      falls

EBB TIDE

Whimbrel Cottage, rescued from a series of nor'easters, has a new south deck, a shelter from north winds that often blow on my autumn and spring retreats. Settling into the May sun, I seem to melt into the familiar sea-meets-sky atmosphere while gentle waves whirlpool each piling that elevates the cottage above ghost crabs, shore birds and passersby.

From here I can see all the way up and down the beach and to the horizon. In the distance, where the cottages end and the wildlife refuge begins, the silhouette of a woman walking a dog comes into view, her skirts billowing gently. I turn back to face the sea, meditating awhile, the ocean's deep breaths measuring mine. When I open my eyes, I notice the woman will soon pass below me and I smile, anticipating hers . . .

>   ebb tide ~
>   her seeing-eye dog
>   sets the pace

WHIMBREL COTTAGE REVISITED

After Father's dying I abandon all, retreat to the isolated cottage by the shore that so often has lifted me in times of darkness . . .

    soft knock on the door
    a pause in the ocean
    startles me

I peer through sea-smeared windows and find an elderly man with a lost look on his face and a brightly-colored tourist map fluttering in his hands . . .

    a missed turn
    off a trail of lighthouses ~
    his arrival at my door

Was this, then, the *I Ching's* meaning I had just cast at dawn? Unity, Coordination . . . of what, I wondered . . . should I join this lonely man, show him places on this barrier island where nature's secrets offer more light than any beacon could . . .

    small arch of a rainbow
    turned upside down
    cradles the noonday sun

small time

The seaside cottage where I once found solitude and respite from the world was demolished by Hurricane Floyd. Now the neighboring cottage that once stood well back from the tideline is in danger of being taken by the next big storm. Yet I'm relieved to have this alternate retreat to turn to, and pause from unloading the car to rest on the deck awhile, remembering my first spring along this narrow strip of the Outer Banks, bordered by ocean and sound . . .

>moonpath—
>the glitter of thrashing fish
>sifted through it

Washing a few dishes, I watch a small-time fishing operation from my cottage window; nets are hauled by a hand-turned crank that sits in the back of a rusty pick-up, the tide gently pulling packed sand from around its back wheels. Their catch seems slight this moonrise and later, just before bed, I check on their progress again . . .

>moonclouds—
>a man and a woman
>asleep at the wheel

As I make morning coffee I see that once again the nets have been dragged to shore . . .

>rainbow of scales
>through brightly colored mesh—
>laundry baskets

An early walker and her dog pause to watch the baskets being loaded onto the bed of the truck, a bountiful catch that overflows. Before driving off, the couple canvass the beach for spilled fish, but a few are missed . . .

                      over the ones that got away
                            her black lab
                            paws to the sky

MOON WATCH

The coolness of damp sand against the soles of my feet in the darkness almost the feeling of floating on the calm sea beside me each rise and fall of waves as soothing as the heartbeat of a mother against her child's resting head. So tempting to recline and sleep on this beach where just two months ago we witnessed the excavation of a deep pit created by the hind flippers of a loggerhead turtle . . .

        summer solstice ~
        moist pearly eggs drop
        through the torch's red beam

Along Cape Hatteras National Seashore a scattering of these ocean-dwelling reptiles still seek out island beaches in what has become a quest of survival for this threatened species. Enduring sweltering days and humid nights, shifts of park rangers, interns and volunteers guard the mounded nest throughout the summer . . .

        shades of twilight ~
        the fox's sidewinding gait
        along the shore

Now, under an August moon that casts a rippling path from horizon to shore, the turtle patrol waits in silence until at last a hundred hatchlings struggle out of their shells, then turn instinctively toward the shining trail that will lead them through the surf to their home . . . between six pairs of bare feet, outstretched flippers flail awkwardly, propelling bodies small enough to fit in a child's palm up tiny hillocks of sand

and down again as though willing to scale mountains in their trek to the sea . . .

      the faintest tinkle ~
      glittery seashell fragments
      turn with the tide

Spring Planting

Not far from the tourist-trade beaches of North Carolina, agricultural fields are worked by farm families who not only turn their legacy of rich, dark soil, but also preserve a shaded graveyard in the midst of growing cotton, soybeans or corn. These small, square cemeteries are kept well trimmed and regularly adorned with fresh wreathes of flowers. In a field near our small property there is a plot more elaborately decorated than most, with a white picket fence, painted cut-outs of religious figures and a carved wooden replica of a cathedral, spires and all . . .

>fresh black earth
>circling Jesus and Mary
>the tractor with chipped red paint

AFIELD

CITY PARK

How many times we escaped there: a small urban park bordered on one side by a littered stream trickling its way to an inlet blighted by many years of pollution. Misplaced rocks trucked in from mountainous roads serve as jetties where once wetlands blossomed out, unbroken by paved causeways traversed by busy traffic. As we gaze across this dismal cityscape a great white egret appears, like a ghost lingering from a time when the only disturbance was the splash of a fish or frog ...

        wetlands—
        the great egret's plumes
        grace a tire

ALLIGATOR RIVER WILDLIFE REFUGE

The winter visitors we seek spring up from grasses tangled in shades of tan and wheat that spill from ditches dividing fallow fields from the unpaved roads we bird from. Swamp sparrows, song sparrows, savannah sparrows, like the elusive Lincoln's sparrow we seek, vanish into habitat their plumage so perfectly matches. A male harrier comes into view, coasting low over stubble and matted vegetation that stretches into the distance, his ghostly-grey back easy to track . . .

    the shortest day
    rippling rays of sun
    ink-black wing tips flare

We ride and stop and scan until my eyes blur with achromatic patterns shifting past the lens of my binoculars . . . then, my husband's urgent tap on my shoulder . . .

    old logging road ~
    a blue heron's lift-off
    above a red wolf's leap

I focus on his radio collar as the wolf watches his lost prey glide into a stand of nearby pines, a bough of needles bouncing slightly beneath its weight as it lands. Privileged to witness the reintroduction of this endangered canine 20 years ago, we stalk one of their descendants, slowly edging the mini-van forward, hoping the vehicle will serve as a blind. In shared excitement we lock eyes, and in that brief moment the wolf is gone. We approach the intersection of dusty roads where the wolf stood, careful not to slam doors as we creep out we speak in whispers . . .

> sudden gust ~
> a set of paw prints
> blows over our shoes

Turning our backs now to the swampy thicket that lies opposite fields and drainage ditch, we renew our pursuit of Lincoln's sparrows and hawks. At last we manage to decipher one of the sparrows perched on a bare twig protruding from a patch of bayberry. When we return to the van where hot coffee waits, both of us try to muster enthusiasm for this rare winter bird, whose addition to our life list seems somewhat of an anticlimax to the red wolf. We remove padded hats and gloves, still cautiously quiet about sliding open the side door as we prepare to stash our belongings for the ride home. Yet something makes me turn for one final look, a vague flutter of danger in my gut . . .

> wind parts the reeds ~
> golden eyes of the wolf
> watching us

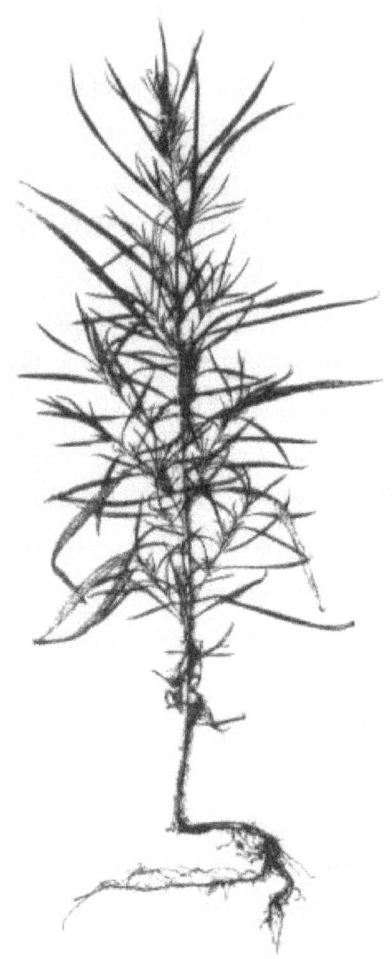

South Texas

Flashing pink crescent moons with each beat of their wings, scissor-tailed flycatchers thrill us as they launch from high wires lining the long straight road to Santa Ana. We scan fields irrigated with water from the Rio Grande, searching for the odd hawk or perhaps a roadrunner dashing from nearby scrubs. Accustomed to birding along the Atlantic Flyway, we soon adapt to the unfamiliarity of resacas, retama trees and mesquite, whose willow-like limbs drape over green jays instead of blue. Entering the wildlife refuge in dawn's coolness, we follow sinuous trails to a wind-ruffled lake where a pair of whistling ducks balance precariously atop their nest box, hot-pink bills touching . . .

>   a part in the cattails ~
>   Spanish moss brushes
>   a Border Patrol jeep

A few more sightings even at dusk as we load birding books and binoculars into the car we anticipate microwave dinners, an evening in our air-conditioned room talking over the day as we add Texas birds to our list in the laptop. The return trip a little hurried at first, then we slow down to view the moon rising over orange groves and mobile homes with makeshift awnings tacked on by the people who live and work among them . . .

>   pausing over twin washboards
>   a migrant wife's eyes
>   lifted to the moon

Mesa Verde, Colorado

Circling up through soft rock colored in shades of fading sunset, I feel loosened granules waft my face in a light breeze, revealing shapes sculpted by the wind . . . shifting art as holes fall out and fill in. Desert lizards too carve out their designs . . . puffed in territorial displays they tap out tiny crevices with delicate toes, raining tinted sandstone to the path below.

Ascending to the level top I look down at ancient homes caved from sheer cliffs, their artifacts carefully arranged by archeological expertise. Lost in the mystery of these hills, I gaze across the chasm to the other side and find you standing there, as though we had never parted, as though you had waited in this timeless place all this time, ready to forgive my betrayal, holding my remorse in your hands.

Could it have been you and you didn't know? Like how the dead are sighted by one whose love cannot bear the sundering? I severed you without thought or heart, fearing inevitable change, trying to outrun fate's inevitable blows . . . then there he stood, this man, so perfectly you staring back at me, deserted dwellings at our feet as though to mock my emptiness . . .

>   chasm between us
>   last fragments of my heart
>   splintered
>   your dear sweet image
>   now only in my dreams

PIGEON MOUNTAIN

As I cross the one-lane bridge a few cattle pause to glance up at me from the swiftly-flowing creek below, then amble up the bank to the monastery's pasture. A sharp curve leads me up from the creek bed, and I feel the weight of built-up tension fall in a rush as the familiar bell tower emerges between tree tops . . .

> low glide of turkeys
> down the slope of a field
> gentle toll of bells

At the foot of the convent's walkway I stop for a moment and scan the rolling hill below me, searching for the huge old apple tree whose fruit I know will be gathered by nuns and deer in the fall. I find it toppled by a recent storm, its ridge of dark roots protruding from the earth . . .

> shades of twilight
> a pale crown of blossoms
> whitening

Pressing the visitor's bell, I silently give thanks for the ancient traditions of this Cistercian Order, who provide solitude for those seeking refuge from the distractions and demands of the day-to-day world. Sister Claire, currently assigned retreatant duties, appears at the top half of the Dutch door where I wait, as instructed by a faded notice posted on the wall . . .

> Rocksport-shod
> sister in traditional
> black and white
> . . . age-old blessing
> and embrace

An old farm gate locked behind me, I drive slowly up a gravel road that leads to the retreat cabin isolated on a rise overlooking a pond and the stone remains of an 18th-century ice house. My favorite handwritten sign is still in its place by the door . . .

> hermitage rules:
> when Sister cuts the grass
> please refrain
>   from speaking
>   unnecessarily

And this is why I come: silence for five days without telephone, television or computer. Immediately I sit zazen, the spirit of this place caressing mine . . .

> just after sunset
> the raucous signaling
> of Canada geese

The rustic three-room cabin is equipped with a wood stove and has a small rotating library stocked by the sisters and retreatants. A crucifix hangs over my single bed, yet the reading material reflects a diversity of teachings on meditation and prayer from Sister Teresa to Krisnamurti.

I find a small round of gouda in the refrigerator—the livelihood of these dozen or so nuns whose cheese barn adjoins their convent. A loaf of bread from a Trappist monastery is also provided . . .

> hands joined in labor ~
> flavor of a simple meal
> intensified

Darkness settles more suddenly in these mountains than it does along our coastal plain, and I eagerly crawl into bed knowing from past visits how quickly my whole being slips into the cycle of meditation, study and simple chores this contemplative order follows, as though attuned to the biorhythms nature intended. The geese too have quieted for the night and sleep comes almost instantly . . .

> echoes
> of monastery bells
> awaken me
> in my cabin retreat
> ghostly taps against the wall

When the bell for matins stops I listen for the odd noise I thought came from just outside . . . how soon silence has released my hidden fears! I raise the window shade to reassure myself that my solitude remains undisturbed . . .

> 3 a.m.
> crossing the dew-covered lawn
> glow of the full moon

Bracing my back against the rough log wall behind my bed I begin to focus on my breath, somehow reassured by the idea that the sisters too are meditating in their rooms . . .

> in stillness of night
> solitary moan of wind
> rising and falling

Walking meditation at dawn, my legs adjusting to the steepness of the rocky mountain paths—such a change from the flatlands I'm accustomed to . . .

> morning mist wavers
> only the caw of the crow
> crosses the pond

At the crest of the trail the faint trickle of a nearby creek and countersongs of birds lighting up the hills . . .

> orchard oriole ~
> the whole body throb
> of his song

My afternoon alternates with periods of writing, reading and meditation. I try mindfully washing dishes as advised by Thich Nhat Hanh. Later, I take the mile walk to the cloister, then follow signs to the visitors section of the small chapel where vespers will be sung. Concerned that I might arrive late and interrupt the service, I find I have instead arrived early . . .

> smoldering wax
> in the empty chapel
> a kneeling pad creaks

Soon the sisters file silently in . . . then lost to my view in their private corner of this sacred place . . .

> not knowing
> this weight had become
> so heavy . . .
> the nuns' chant at vespers
> unstoppable tears

On my last morning I sweep the cabin, strip linens from the bed and bag up my small bit of trash. After dropping these off in the convent's parlor per instructions, I leave my car radio turned off, relishing a final period of silence. I'm grateful for a cool, cloudy day, allowing me to keep the car windows closed against the traffic.

> four days of silence
> in the old log cabin
> ~ my mind
>   haunted yet
>   by those it released

Merchants Millpond State Park, NC

Our first spring day on Merchants Millpond . . . we paddle leisurely around tupelo trees whose trunks sprout from the water in the classic shape of closed a lotus . . . an orchard oriole sits atop its canopy, his black, monk-like hood shimmering in the sunlight as he warbles his mating song. Blue-gray gnatcatchers nip lichens from tupelo branches, forming them into a nest the size of a doll's teacup, then with a belly shimmy and cheerful calls, the mated pair take turns rounding out their creation. Stately bald cypress trees also grace the millpond, adorned with Spanish moss that grazes our canoe as we maneuver among the knee-like protrusions of their roots . . .

> veil of tendriled moss ~
> a drake snips a blossom
> of spatterdock

The decayed stumps of more ancient cypress—some as old as a thousand years—serve as hosts to blueberry bushes, pink swamp roses and pines which naturally take on bonsai shapes in their odd containers. Drifting around the next weathered snag we spot a sleek body ahead of us trailing a small wake that gently braids into itself as the animal slinks out of the water and disappears into the dark cavity of the next cypress stump . . .

> distant thunder ~
> a flash of light
> from the mink's creamy neck

About the Author

A native of Washington, D.C., Linda Jeannette Ward spent the summers of her childhood on her grandparents' Maryland farm where her love of nature was nurtured. She currently lives along the North Carolina coast where she and her husband maintain twenty acres of woods and swamp as a wildlife refuge. She regularly birds the Outer Banks of N.C., a group of barrier islands that attract a wide range of species.

Linda Jeannette Ward is best known for her tanka poetry, published in journals internationally, and included in two collections: *A Frayed Red Thread* (Clinging Vine Press, 2000) and *Scent of Jasmine and Brine* (Inkling Press, 2007). Strongly influenced by traditional Japanese forms, her haiku, tanka and haibun are often written in a modern style favored by English-language poets. She was presented with a first prize for haiku (British Haiku Society) and tanka (Tanka Society of America) in 2009.

About the Artists

Pamela A. Babusci has been watercolor painting since college and sumi-e painting for the past four years. She has been pressing flowers/ferns/leaves/wild grasses for over 25 years. Her art and illustrations have graced the covers and interior pages of *Chiyo's Corner, Persimmon, Heron Quarterly of Haiku and Zen Poetry, RAW NerVZ HAIKU, South by Southeast, Oneself, A Harvest of Haiku,* and *Full Moon Tide: The Best of Tanka Splendor 1990-1999*. At Haiku North America 2001, an international conference held in Boston, Massachusetts, she was awarded first place during a haiga workshop. Pamela teaches haiku, tanka, haiga, sumi-e painting and kanji symbols to elementary and high school students independently and through the Artists-In-Residence program in Rochester, New York. Her sumi-e art has been selected for four issues of the Haiku Society of America's newsletter, and recently was chosen as the logo for Haiku North America 2003, New York City. Pamela is also an internationally accomplished haiku and tanka poet. She won the *Museum of Haiku Literature Award* in 1995 and Tanka Splendor Awards 1996-1999 and 2001.

J.W. Stansell, a South Carolina native, now lives in Norfolk, Virginia. His mixed media art has been exhibited there as part of the Tidewater Artists Society's *Cutting Edge* art show and at Tidewater Community College. He illustrated the cover for the compact disk *Mixed Media* in 1999. This is his first publication of pen and ink drawings for a collection of poetry.

www.ingramcontent.com/pod-product-compliance
Lightning Source LLC
Chambersburg PA
CBHW020022050426
42450CB00005B/602